How to Write a Book in a Week.
A Writer's Guide to Meeting a Deadline

By Johanne R. Deschamps
©2016

Table of Contents

Introduction

> People on the outside think there's something magical about writing, that you go up in the attic at midnight and cast the bones and come down in the morning with a story, but it isn't like that. You sit in back of the typewriter and you work, and that's all there is to it.
>
> –Harlan Ellison

Writing a book can <u>seem</u> daunting. I emphasize the word, <u>seem</u> because, in reality, all you have to do is write. The problem with the writing process, for most people is not that they can't write. It's usually a variety of other factors such as feeling that they don't have the time to put in or they are lacking motivation. Another famous line is, "I'll write that book as soon as I get a great idea." Or, they have an idea but they are unsure of the process and do not have a method with which to approach the task.

Here is the bottom line. Most aspiring writers have no shortage of ideas. Most people can make some time to write, and with the technology and resources available today, anyone can do research. The secret to writing and finishing a writing project is in two main components.

1) How you look at the art of writing.
2) How you look at yourself.

Transform these elements into action and you will have a finished book. I can't promise that you will write a best seller. What I can say is that you will learn how and what it takes to complete your writing projects. I warn you in advance that you will have to work hard to accomplish this. But if you follow all of the advice, it works.

Your own pace may be different so allow yourself the time you need. You may be working on a very large writing project but the same process will get you the results you want. Whatever your goal is, bear in mind that you will then have to see it through; so be realistic about the time frame you impose on yourself. Happy Writing!

Time Is On Your Side

Amateurs sit and wait for inspiration, the rest of us get up and go to work

-Stephen King

Some people use time, or lack of time as an excuse for delaying or not finishing a book or a writing project. The methods that I talk about in this book can be adapted and used by anyone, even people who lead very busy lives or have hectic schedules and time constraints. You just have to prepare in advance by using some or all of the following helpful tips that I have found useful. Because you have such a hectic schedule, you may not write your book in a week but perhaps you can write it in a month. If you set a realistic goal for yourself based on your lifestyle, there is always a way.

Firstly, inform your friends and family that you will be unavailable to take calls or visit during the hours that you are working. There will be plenty of time to return calls or messages later. There are also many time-wasting activities in which we tend to get caught up on a daily basis. We don't even realize how much of our time these consume. Before you know it, an hour or a half a day has been wasted when you add up all of the time consumed by these distractions. These time wasters may not be the same for everyone but the result is the same. Here are some examples of what I consider to be time-wasters. Watching television listening to radio or music, if it distracts you or takes you off task. You must resist the urge to check email and social media or surf the net. Do not make or take phone calls (you can return calls later, when you have finished your work for the day or during a scheduled break) or text unless it is an emergency. If you are serious about a writing career, you must discipline yourself to avoid these or similar activities while trying to work.

I also recommend keeping a pen and small notebook or any type of paper in your purse or handbag. You can also carry these items in your pocket for men or women who don't like to carry a bag. Notebooks are available in all sizes, so pick the one that is right for you. You should also keep another set of these items in your car, that way if an idea or a thought comes to mind while you are driving, you can jot these things down as soon as you get to your destination. You can also enter these notes using your cell phone's note application or directly into your laptop or tablet. You may also use an audio recording device if that is more practical.

If you are a stay at home parent and are juggling, housework, children and cooking as well as being a chauffeur, personal secretary nurse etc…you can put your helpful tools in strategic locations around your home. This way you will always be prepared when that idea or special sentence or phrase comes to mind. Make notes throughout your day. If you write your rough draft on paper as I do, always make sure to have at least three or four writing utensils and plenty of paper at your immediate disposal. This will help you avoid wasting time going to retrieve these items should you need them. Once you have enough notes relating to your subject matter or idea, you can begin entering all of this information into a computer if you haven't already done so.

Now that we have the <u>how to</u> of writing on a busy schedule, let's look at the when. What opportunities are available in your schedule? If you are a person who gets to work early, you may be able to take five or ten minutes to write then. Breaks and lunch hours are always a good time too and could be very good for breaking up the monotony of your workday. I often write at coffee shops, in waiting rooms or in my car. Parents, you can write while children are napping or sit with them at the table while they eat their breakfast. Notebook in hand, you will always be prepared.

When you put in the time, you can then relax in the knowledge that you have put in a good day's work and are well on your way to achieving your writing goals. Remember to reward yourself with a pat on the back and treat yourself to some time to do exactly what you want to do. It could be a hot relaxing bath, a walk, a run, tea/coffee or drinks with a friend/s.

Another important aspect of finding time to write is how you manage your time. What are your priorities? Family time is an important priority. Watching television is not.

Checking your social media pages suddenly turns into an hour that you could have spent on your writing project. You have to give up immediate gratification in order to reap the rewards of your hard work at a later date, just like getting your paycheck at the end of the week in a traditional job. This is no different. Do the work. Work the plan.

Note: If your book requires interviews, travel, or a lot of research, you will have to adjust your timeline accordingly. Find small blocks of time, and use them to your advantage. Take notes on every idea, sentence, word or vision that comes to mind.

Inspiration (Beating the Block)

Don't try to figure out what other people want to hear from you; figure out what you have to say. It's the one and only thing you have to offer.

-Barbara Kingsolver

You can get ideas from anywhere and everywhere. You can also get them from nowhere. Inspiration is all around us. It can be found in nature and in human nature. You can get inspiration from; an event, a newspaper article, a television show, a child at play, a good deed, a bad deed or a fashion faux pas. Inspiration is just an idea, an expression, a sight, a sound, a texture, a memory. Ideas for writing can come from a wedding or a funeral, a birth or a death, a crazy dream or a nightmare. Anything can provide inspiration. If you don't believe me, try a little experiment. Pick an everyday common object or your pet. Pick something that is near you now. Something simple such as your coffee mug, a chair. It could even be your cat. Just look at it for a few minutes. Now, grab a pen and paper and start to describe it. Describe it in as much detail as you possibly can. Next write down everything that comes to mind when you think about or look at your object or pet. Do you see how much you can do with something so simple? Now these are just basics but we tend to forget just how simple it can be. Sometimes inspiration just comes to us. Other times you have to look for it, create it.

Here is another example of how to write when your mind is blank. Pick a word. Any word. Now, one at a time, write down every other word that comes into your mind. Some of the words will have relevance to your original word, but some won't. These could then lead to other ideas. These are just a couple of exercises that have helped to pull me out of more than one writer's block.

Treat writing like a job. That's what it is. Don't just sit there with a blank sheet of paper waiting for inspiration to strike. The Ten Commandments won't suddenly appear before you on stone tablets. You are the creator. You are the writer. So, Write! Now, that being said, there are always days and times when you do not have the motivation to write. This is when free writing becomes your best friend. You can just spew onto the page. Worry about the clean up later. It is such a freeing experience. No plan. No rules. No neatness. No worries. Just splash your words everywhere onto the page. Don't worry about whether or not it makes sense or is trite or dull or done to death. Just do it. You would be surprised at the ideas and inspiration that can come from this process!

K.I.S.S. (Keep It Simple Stupid)

In character, in manner, in style, in all things, the supreme excellence is simplicity.

-Henry Wadsworth Longfellow

The length of this book is purposely short because I wanted to illustrate that writing is not rocket science. The steps to success are simple, and it is simply a matter of doing the work to get your book finished. One common belief among successful (published) writers is that it is work. You have to let go of the romantic notions in your head about living the life of a writer. It is hard work and the very first and most important step to becoming a successful writer is to just sit down and write. It doesn't matter what. Write what pleases you. Write what saddens you or angers you. Tell a story. Tell your story or someone else's. Make one up. None of it matters really. All that matters is that you write and that you keep on writing. And for God's sake, be intimate! That's what people want. Go ahead and make it personal. It will be more authentic than telling the story in a robotic way.

Some writers prefer to create an outline before they begin. This is an example of the writer leading the writing and is a method best used by super organized people. If this method works for you, great! I prefer to let the writing lead me. Whatever thoughts are in my mind are what I begin with. Just because you do not think in a linear fashion does not mean that you can't write a book. I am one of these people. It could start with a word, a sentence or just some abstract idea which I feel compelled to put down on paper.

When starting this project, I asked myself, "Is it possible to write a book in a week?" The answer was obvious. There was only one way to find out. Try it and see if my own method would work. So I grabbed a notebook and a pen, seriously, that is all you need. Some people find it easier to type directly into their computer's word processing program. There is no doubt that those who prefer this method will save a lot of time in the process. If you prefer, you can even do your rough draft using an audio recording device if that is more convenient for you. Any method will do as long as you express the ideas that need to be covered.

In order to write a book in a week, you will need to have an un-edited first draft, completed in about one to two days. Next you will need to decide; what are the main points that you want to focus on? Make list of these so that you will be sure to cover the basics. Just one or two words will do. This list will help motivate more thoughts on the subject. In my note book, I usually write these on the back of the previous page. During the free writing portion of this project, you can then go into as much detail as you want about each of these main points. Again, the main idea is to keep writing. You can do it! You will feel excited as you watch the pieces of the puzzle come together to form a cohesive whole.

You will have such a feeling of accomplishment when your book is finished. Just follow the simple instructions and you will be well on your way.

Once you have accomplished your goal, you will be able to move on to the next steps, proof-reading, editing and publication.

Ego

I went for years not finishing anything.
Because, of course, when you finish
something you can be judged.

-Erica Jong

If your goal is to write, you can. The secret is to not let your ego get in the way. Ego and lack of self-confidence are frequent roadblocks to finishing a writing project. Using the methods in this book, you can learn how to overcome both of these deterrents. Even while writing this book, I stopped several times during my free writing and wondered to myself whether my content was too simplistic, too juvenile, too uninspired and therefore who would want to read it. This is one of the hardest obstacles. You must let go of these thoughts as soon as you can. Push them aside and keep on writing. Writing is easier than we think. We, as adults make it much harder than it has to be. We make it harder by expecting perfection of ourselves. We make it harder by being self-conscious. Children are not self- conscious. They have not yet developed the giant egos that we, adults, tend to develop. In order for your project to be successful, you must let go of ego.

Fear is directly tied into ego. After starting a writing project, many new writers will ask themselves, "Why would anyone want to read this? What qualifies me to tell this story?" The answer is because I am daring to write it. It's just that simple. Forget any negative thoughts about your talent or your writing ability. Whether these are self-talk or someone else's judgments.

People in your life may ask you, "What qualifies you to write this book?" If you listen to those people, you won't write your book. You have to believe in yourself. Deep inside, you have to know that you are good enough, smart enough, YOU have to know that you are capable of writing your book and telling the story you want to tell.

I advocate education and getting as much as you can of it. That being said, I want to tell you that lack of education or any formal training is not a roadblock to becoming a successful writer unless you allow it to be. Willa Cather said, "Most of the material a writer works with is acquired before the age of fifteen." I quite agree. As long as you can tell a story, get your point across, impart information and make it entertaining, you can be a writer. You just have to learn how to capture and hold the reader's attention. For this, practice makes perfect. Reading a wide range of material will help you enormously as a writer. You will learn to identify what you consider to be good writing vs. bad writing. It will also give you a feel for what's out there and what sells.

I have read many books which I found disappointing and boring, yet they have been published so someone must find them entertaining or informative. There is something out there for everyone.
Writing is putting your thoughts down on paper and then organizing them into a cohesive whole. There are many tools for managing these steps. Even if you do not have confidence in your writing abilities you can dictate your story and have someone else do the physical act of writing it. You can do your revisions in the same way.

Don't ever let anyone tell you that you can't write because of a lack of formal education. Some people would have you think that this is rocket science. I dare to disagree. And, so should you!

Don't listen to naysayers. As a matter of fact, if you are surrounded by these types of people, don't even tell them that you are writing a book. They will try to discourage you. Perhaps, out of jealousy or ignorance but most likely, because they themselves do not see how it can be done. They do not understand the writing process and think it's much more complicated than it actually is.

You need to avoid this kind of negativity at all cost. As a matter of fact, you need to associate yourself with like-minded people. They are the ones who will understand you and be a more positive influence. Change your lifestyle to include attending writer's conferences or workshops or take a class. These are ways that you can find other writers. Most importantly, if you want to be a writer.....WRITE!

Use your own voice as a writer. Don't try to be someone else or to sound like anyone else. Your voice is what will make your work special.

It is also important that you get used to rejection. Look at each and every rejection slip as a stepping stone toward your ultimate goal of publication. Be confident in your own work and abilities. It is rarely perfection but you can get close as you proceed through the revision process. Be proud of your own work. Take pride in the way you express yourself and don't let a lack of self-confidence get in the way.

I Like It Rough (The First Draft)

The first draft of anything is shit.

-Ernest Hemingway

One simple way to look at writing is that it is just an expression of thought. Therefore, if you keep your mind on whatever subject matter you want to write about, you can then write down all of your thoughts on this subject. For me the process of writing a rough draft can best be described as a purging. A purging of my soul, of my knowledge and of my emotions pertaining to the subject I am writing about. Once it's all on paper the purging is over and I feel better.

This is where it begins. Don't worry about what you are saying. Just write down everything you know or want to say about the subject. Write fast and write furiously. Write as if this is your last chance to get everything down on paper. You should not be concerned about a beginning, a middle and an end. In other words, you should not be worried about the order in which you are writing down the thoughts and/or events that you put on paper. This worrying about the details will only hamper your efforts at creativity as well as your ability to complete your project.

Several times during the writing of this book, I stopped, momentarily, worried about whether or not I was using the exact word that I wanted to use. I caught myself. I knew that I wanted to use a different word to express my thought, but to stop and reflect on this now, or to get out a thesaurus or look something up on the internet is a major no-no. To stop and do research in the middle of free writing your first draft usually will take you off track This can delay or possibly derail you from the completion of your book. The hesitation was only for a moment. When you catch yourself doing this, tell yourself, "NO."

You may even lose interest after writing for a while but you must resist the urge to stop writing. Keep writing. As long as <u>you</u> understand what it is that you want to say. Do not edit along the way. I cannot emphasize this enough. Do not throw anything out until after the final editing process. The rest goes into the editing time, later. We must dare to play! Play with words, with ideas. We must play with sights, sounds and imagination.

Some people find it easier to type directly into their computer's word processing program. Some people use paper and pencil for their rough draft. I've done both but feel I am able to be more creative when using pen and paper. Yes! I said pen. I dare to use a pen for my first draft. Because it's only for me. I find that when using a pencil I am more tempted to use an eraser and try to edit as I go along. Again, A major faux pas. A time wasting proposition. Do not, I repeat…do not edit anything as you write. It doesn't matter if I later cross things out during the editing process. I also prefer the boldness of ink. Dare to say what you want to say. No restrictions, no worrying
about grammar; punctuation, spelling, or syntax. Just write! Everything can be modified later. Let your mind just cut loose with everything you want to say on the subject.

Other stuff may creep in. That's ok too. During the editing process you can choose to cut out whatever you want. The material that you edit out can be temporarily put into a "parking lot."(A separate file where you could park these thoughts and ideas for possible use in the future. Maybe your next book if it doesn't belong in this one.

Using this method of free writing, you should be able to write about three pages every ten minutes. Even if you average five minutes per page, you should be able to write 12 pages per hour. Before you know it your first draft will be completed. You can later, supplement what you have written with a few hours of research on the subject matter you are writing about, or you can do another free-writing session. Add this new found knowledge to your existing manuscript and you have a rough draft.

After only five pages into my free writing for the rough draft of this project, my arm began to get sore, not from writing too much, but from writing so fast. This is part of the secret. Try to get your thoughts down on paper as quickly as you can, before your brain has a chance to censor what you are writing. That is a task reserved for later during the editing process.

There is an expression that I heard from my boss during my time working in sales. "If you throw enough shit on the wall, some of it's going to stick." This applies to writing too.

If you need to take a short break during your free writing sessions, take one. Just try to avoid doing this too frequently. The goal is to keep your mind on the subject matter that you are writing about. Don't get lost in other thoughts.

After 14 pages of my free writing exercise, my hand was beginning to swell. Now, some of you may think this is ludicrous. But, think for a moment, if you worked in a warehouse; if you worked as a cashier or a waitress, you would probably have a sore back or sore legs at the end of your shift. So too might there may be pain or discomfort as a result of writing in this manner. If you are typing directly into your word processing program, your eyes may get sore, your back or butt may get tired of being in the same position for too long. Being a writer does not mean a free ride. It's just a different kind of work. Also, make sure to eat when you are working this intensely. Your brain needs fuel. Waste no time during the free writing session of your rough draft.

Do The Puzzle (Making it Legible)

It's none of their business that you have to learn to write. Let them think you were born that way.

-Ernest Hemingway

Once your rough draft is completed, it must be entered into your word processor so you can put the pieces together. For me, this is the most exciting part of the process. This is where you begin to see your piece taking shape. I liken this process to doing a jigsaw puzzle and I approach it in a similar way. Just as in solving a jigsaw puzzle, you start by finding the top, the bottom, the sides and the middle. Matching colors and content go together. From here it is trial and error until all of the pieces fit. At this point you should have a picture that is fairly complete.

Your next step will be to re-read what you have written. During this step you will also be moving things around and putting them into the proper order. You may choose to add to or remove certain content as you do so. During this part of the process you will no doubt, find gaps that you should fill with any pertinent information which you feel may be missing.

Once this is done, you should have a clearer picture of how you can / should divide your ideas up using the main points that we discussed in Chapter 4.

Now that you have organized your book by separating the main points or ideas, start dividing these ideas up into different chapters using the main theme of each idea. Re-read again, adding everything you have written on that specific idea or subject into the appropriate chapters.

After working with your rough draft, adding to it and expanding it, you will see many gaps. Rather than trying to fill each one singularly, try doing another free writing session. Often, this will supply a lot of the missing pieces in your puzzle.

As you are re-reading what you have written, ask yourself, "How does this sound to me?" Avoid using words just to try to impress your reader. Just get to the point you are trying to make. It is better to show your reader using an example rather than trying to baffle them with lengthy explanations. Re-writing is important. Do it as often as you think is necessary to achieve the desired result.

Polishing the Silver (The Editing Process)

It is perfectly okay to write garbage—as long as you edit brilliantly.

-C. J. Cherryh

Once you have all of your work from your rough draft divided into the appropriate sections, you can now really begin to get into, what I call, the polishing of your book. Now you should be checking for errors in grammar as well as spelling and punctuation. As you are re-reading and re-writing in this step, pay special attention to how the words, sentences and paragraphs flow. If you find that a certain word or phrase that you've used doesn't accurately convey what you want to say, this is the time to fix it. Get out your thesaurus or dictionary and play around with different alternatives. Pay attention to meaning and context but also to how it sounds or flows as you read. Writing, after all, is an art. If you want your reader to be interested in what you have to say, you have to be conscious of how you say it as well. Just as a visual artist is concerned with presentation, so should you be as a writer.

The final step is to re-read and re-write if necessary one final time, making sure to look for the smallest errors. Have someone else read it if you are not sure of your editing skills. This is a good idea anyway because a fresh set of eyes will often catch things that we may have missed.

Three re-writes should be all that is necessary to have a good finished project. Though you can do more if you feel that is required to meet your own standards. Just don't procrastinate too much at this step or your efforts at perfection will sometimes end with ego scrapping the project.

You should now have a finished book that you can either submit to a publisher or you can decide to self-publish If you are submitting for publication, bear in mind that you may be asked to make further changes as everyone has their own criteria for publication.

A Final Word

The work never matches the dream of perfection the artist has to start with.

-William Faulkner

Many aspiring writers are waiting for inspiration to strike so they can be creative. I myself was guilty of this for years, not knowing the truth. With no formal training, I relied on inspiration to fuel my passion. The reality is that your passion has to fuel your work. It is work. What most people don't understand, and what I have learned after years of wasted time was that the bottom line is, writing is a job. Like any other job. It requires many hours of dedication and discipline to complete writing projects. The only difference is that you are the boss and the worker. If you are lucky, then you love your job. Many people go off every day to jobs which they do not love or are unfulfilling. Yet, somehow they manage to do it. They do their work and they get through each day, one day at a time. They don't call the boss and say, "Sorry, I'm uninspired today. As soon as the inspiration hits me, I'll be in." No, that would result in not having a job. Similarly, if you do not have the self-discipline to write every day, or at least most days, inspired or not, this will result in you not being a published author.

Inspiration can be a great start to a project but you have to dedicate yourself to finishing it. You have to dedicate yourself to looking at each project you start as a job and not just an idea or an inspiration you had during a flash of genius. I can't tell you how many great ideas and inspirations are just sitting in peoples computers or in notebooks, neglected for years when all that is required is some TLC and the discipline to finish the job. Then, and only then, will you begin to see your great ideas come to fruition.

Accomplish your writing goals! Put an end to just starting them and shelving them.This does not mean that you can never put a project aside or let it rest and revisit it later. Many writers do this but if it's all you ever do, you will never finish anything.

The system works. I have proven it by writing this book in just seven days. Depending on the length of your book, and the subject matter, you may have to give yourself more time, but you can lay the foundation using the same method for larger projects as well. Maybe your project will take a month or a couple of months, etc. The point is, that you decide and then stick to your deadline. Yes, your own self-imposed deadline. Just as if it were a deadline given to you by your employer.

Imagine that you are working for a magazine, or your company wants you to produce a book on a certain subject by a certain date. My guess is, you will make that deadline. That is how things get done!

"There is no real ending. It's just the place where you stop the story."

-Frank Herbert

About The Author

Writing has never been a choice for me. It is a love affair that I have had since childhood. I am, therefore, I write. I used to watch my mother writing letters that were pages and pages in length. They seemed to go on forever. I always wondered what secrets they contained. Sometimes, after she fell asleep I would sneak into her room and read them. I remember being so surprised and impressed with how well she was able to express herself. I was amazed at how different her written word sounded from her every day Mommy language. It was beautiful, it was poetic, and it was sheer happiness.

I enjoy solitude but I believe that's also why I love writing. I can be alone with my thoughts. I can share them with that nice clean sheet of the empty page. I have such a compulsion to write that I have even written on dirty table napkins, on the back of cigarette packs, store receipts, etc. You know you are a writer when you simply have to write. I have written poems in five minutes and essays in a day or two.

This book is geared toward aspiring writers, but can also be used by business people who want to write a book to use as a promotional tool for their business or company.

The idea for this book actually came about by accident. I had been using every plausible excuse to explain to myself why I hadn't been writing in over a year. I decided I had to get back to my writing, but it was discouraging because I often have many great ideas but have rarely finished anything.

I spontaneously Googled, <u>How to write a book in a week.</u> While skimming over a few of the search results, I realized that I had the secret all along. I had done this before and with successful results. That is why I looked to the method I had used previously I am not an organized person in the traditional sense. I create my own systems of organization. They make sense to me. So I decided to put my system to the test. An experiment, if you will, to see if I could write a book in a week using my own methods. I promised myself that if I could do it and was satisfied with the result, then I would publish the book so that perhaps other aspiring authors could benefit from this method.

So create a time frame that works for you and just write!

How to Write a Book in a Week

A Writer's Guide to Meeting a Deadline
By Johanne Deschamps

To read more published works by Johanne Deschamps, follow
My Facebook Page

https://www.facebook.com/johannewrites/

 Follow me on Twitter

https://twitter.com/johannewrites